THE FUTURE OF REAL ESTATE MARKETING

Eric Chuang

Copyright © 2025 Eric Chuang

All rights reserved.

ISBN: 9781726881036

Table of Contents

Preface		1
Introduction		3
Chapter 1	Why I'm Writing This Book	7
Chapter 2	Breaking The Real Estate Marketing Myths	12
Chapter 3	The Bond	24
Chapter 4	The Action-Based Branding System Overview	34
Chapter 5	The Bond and The Sales Process	43
Chapter 6	The Responsive Marketing Funnel (RMF)	49
Chapter 7	Campaigns and Entry Points	62
Chapter 8	Retargeting – How To Stay Top of Mind Without Being Annoying	75
Chapter 9	Conclusion and Final Wrap-Up	80

Real estate agents are working harder than ever.
More content. More platforms. More competition.
And yet… many are getting fewer serious leads, not more.

It's not because you're lazy.
It's not because you don't care.
It's not because you're not good at what you do.

It's because the rules of marketing have changed.

The old playbook—just getting your name out there, posting listings, bragging about your sales—is broken.

Today's client doesn't want to be sold to.
They want to feel *understood*.
They want *real help*, not hype.
They want someone who's already earned their trust before the first handshake.

That's what this book is about.

If you follow the system inside this book, you'll no longer need to chase leads.
You'll attract the right people—automatically—and close more deals with less stress.

Instead of working harder for random attention, you'll work smarter to build a system that brings the right people to you.

You won't need to post mindlessly every day.

You won't need to convince cold leads why they should work with you.

You won't need to burn yourself out trying to stay "top of mind."

Instead, you'll finally have a system that:

- Puts you in front of people who are already ready to act
- Builds trust before the conversation even starts
- Lets you do what you do best—guide, advise, and close

This isn't theory.

This is what the best marketers and the biggest platforms already know—and profit from.

You're about to learn how to build it for yourself.

Welcome to the future of real estate marketing.

Let's get started.

INTRODUCTION

This book isn't for everyone.

If you're a real estate agent who just wants to post a few houses on Instagram and hoping for more commission, *this won't help you*.

This book is also not for agents looking for quick hacks or "get deals fast" tricks.

If you're hoping for a secret script that magically turns strangers into closings overnight, save your money and your time.

If you're not looking to provide value and help your clients, please refund this book or gift it to someone who will.

This book is for agents who are ready to build a business, not just a brand. It's for the ones who understand that consistency beats virality—and that systems outperform hustle. It's for the agents who know there are buyers and sellers out there *right now*—and they're looking for someone to guide them. **The question is: will it be you?**

You're probably doing everything "they" said to do:

- Posting daily on Instagram
- Recording videos, reels, maybe even dancing on TikTok

- Hosting open houses that nobody shows up to
- Sending postcards that get tossed before they're read
- Following up with leads who ghost you
- DM'ing strangers just to get left on "seen"

And you're still not getting the right kind of leads—people who are serious, motivated, and ready to act.

You're working hard—but you're marketing to the wrong people, in the wrong way, and probably at the wrong time.

That's because most marketing advice is written for clicks and views—not contracts and closings.

You've been handed a broken playbook.

A playbook built on attention, not action.

And here's the worst part—

Someone else is getting those deals.
Someone who isn't working harder than you.
Just smarter.
Because while you're chasing attention, they're capturing action.

I wrote this book because I saw firsthand how many agents were wasting time and money chasing the wrong kind of attention. I don't come from the real estate world—I came from selling products online. I built online stores, launched products, and figured out how to convert strangers into buyers. And when I got pulled into the real estate space, I saw the exact same patterns—but with way bigger price tags.

That's when it clicked:

If the leads aren't converting, the issue isn't your hustle.
*The issue is who you're marketing to—and **how** you're doing it.*

Agents don't need more exposure.
They need more action.
They need **Action-Based Branding**.

What Is Action-Based Branding?

Action-Based Branding is a real estate marketing strategy built to convert—not just get noticed.

It's branding designed for people already in motion. People who are:

- Touring homes
- Requesting info
- Searching listings
- Getting a mortgage

It's not about building awareness. It's about being there at the moment of action—with the tools, trust, and timing to make the next step easy.

You don't need to convince anyone to buy or sell. You just need to be *available when they're ready to be in the market for real estate* — and already be the agent they want to call.

And I'll show you how.

CHAPTER 1: WHY I'M WRITING THIS BOOK

How do you make you look like the only choice, not just one of many?

Back in 2015, I wasn't thinking about real estate.

I had just left my job developing iPhone apps, was dealing with some personal obligations, and needed something that gave me freedom and flexibility.

By 2017, I was running my own Amazon business—selling physical products online (really niche door hardware produces).

No clients. No agency. Just me, learning how to move products online through listings, funnels, and ads.

I was building ecommerce funnels, writing ad copy, and figuring out how to move products online.

And what I realized quickly was this:

> If your product looks like everyone else's, your only competitive advantage is price.

That's a losing game.

The minute you look like a commodity, you start getting treated like one—and the only way to win is by being cheaper, faster, or louder.

It's a race to the bottom—and the bottom is brutal.

So I stopped focusing on being competitive...
and started focusing on being *the obvious choice*.

And that truth doesn't just apply to selling online. It applies to real estate too.

Everyone looked the same. Said the same things.
"Top agent." "Dream home." "Let me help you."

So naturally, clients (can't blame them) treated them like interchangeable options—shopping based on convenience or cost, not value.

That realization became even clearer when a friend of mine—brand new to real estate—asked for help with her marketing.

She was stuck in that same "commodity loop."

She had the hustle, minimal experience and no traction.

So I helped her reposition.

We didn't focus on her.

We focused on the *client journey*—what buyers were searching for, what sellers were stressing about, and how we could show up at the exact right time with real value.

And it worked.

She started getting calls. Showings. Offers.
All without chasing people or cold messaging leads who weren't ready.

Because when Action-Based Branding is done right, you don't chase clients—
you attract them.
You stop being an option…
and start being the obvious choice.

That's when I knew:
The same marketing principles that sold thousands of door hardwares online could help agents close more deals in real life.

The secret? Stop trying to get everyone's attention—and start showing up for the people who are in the position to buy or sell real estate.

That's what this book is about.

The Shift That Changes Everything

Most agents are taught to market for attention.
But attention doesn't pay the bills—closings do.

The agents who win in today's market aren't just louder.
They're *smarter*.
They build systems that show up at the exact right time.
They serve instead of sell.
They simplify instead of pitch.
They stop chasing—and start closing.

This book is your roadmap to becoming *that* kind of agent.

Whether you're a solo agent, a small team, or someone trying to break into the top 5%, you'll learn how to:

- Build a marketing system that attracts action-takers
- Position yourself as the obvious choice (and only choice)
- Fill your pipeline with qualified leads
- Do it all without burning out, selling out, or selling your soul

And if you do it right, with a little bit of luck, you'll have clients coming to you.

Let's get to it.

What You'll Walk Away With

By the time you finish this book, you'll understand the Action-Based Branding system.
You'll know how to set it up once—so it works for you over and over again.

It will show you how to:

- Attract serious, motivated leads without chasing
- Build trust *before* someone enters the market
- Create marketing that works while you sleep
- Shift from cold outreach to **inbound interest**

This isn't about short-term tricks.
It's about long-term systems.

Systems that bring you leads.
Systems that build relationships before the conversation even starts.
Systems that free up your time while keeping your pipeline full.

If you're ready for that—keep reading.

Let's build something that actually works.

CHAPTER 2: BREAKING THE REAL ESTATE MARKETING MYTHS

Where everyone else is doing it wrong—and how that creates your advantage.

This chapter is here to clear the air.

Before we can show you how the Action-Based Branding system actually works, we need to remove the mental blocks and bad advice that are probably holding you back.

You might already know some of this. You might not.

Feel free to skip this chapter if you're ready to get into the strategy—I've kept it as short as possible. But I felt it was necessary to call out these false beliefs so we can eliminate any barriers to your success.

If you've ever said,
"I tried that marketing stuff and it didn't bring me any business…"
then this chapter is for you.

Because it's not that marketing doesn't work.
It's that you were taught to use it *wrong*.

Most of the "advice" floating around the real estate world right now is either outdated, misapplied, or just plain backwards.

It sounds good.
It feels productive.
But it doesn't move the needle.

In fact, a lot of it actually creates more frustration—because it keeps you working hard without getting anywhere.

But here's the good news:
Every broken belief in this industry is an opportunity.

If you can see where everyone else is wasting time and energy… and you build a smarter system that does the *right* things at the *right* time…
you win.

Myth #1: Marketing = Getting Leads

This is the biggest misconception—and the one that costs agents the most.

Most people think marketing is about getting leads.
As long as the phone rings or the form gets filled, the marketing worked... right?

Wrong.

Here's the truth:
Marketing is a two-part process.
And most agents are only doing the first part.

Step 1: Attract Attention

This is what most lead gen strategies focus on.
Run an ad. Make a post. Offer a free home valuation.
Get someone to click or reach out.

☑ You've generated a lead.

But that doesn't mean you've earned the deal.

Because attention isn't trust.
And trust is what gets contracts signed.

Step 2: Build the Bond

This is where the real work (and the real money) happens.

Once someone shows interest, they enter a second phase:
They're watching. Comparing. Judging. Thinking.

"Do I like this person?"
"Do they feel credible?"
"Would I actually trust them with my money, my move, my future?"

That's where most agents fall off.

They expect the lead to call them back.
They expect one ad or one landing page to do all the heavy lifting.

But the second step—what we call **Indoctrination (or Bond Building)**—is where the real conversion happens.

And the agents who have a system for it?
They win.

They don't just get leads.
They turn leads into relationships—and relationships into closings.

Myth #2: You Need to Post Every Day to Stay Relevant

You've heard it:

"You've got to stay top of mind. Just keep posting!"

So you try to keep up:

Reels, Stories, behind-the-scenes, Just Listed, Just Sold, market stats, memes, maybe even a trending audio.

But eventually… you burn out.

Because posting every day with no strategy is exhausting and ineffective.

And here's why:

The algorithm doesn't reward effort—it rewards relevance.

Your audience doesn't care how often you post—they care about whether it's helpful, timely, or interesting to *them*.

So instead of posting every day, build a system that delivers the **right message to the right person at the right time.**

That's what Action-Based Branding does.

It replaces the hamster wheel with a system.

You're no longer guessing.

You're guiding.

Myth #3: Listings Are Your Best Marketing Asset

This one is sneaky because it *feels* logical.

You've got a listing—it looks great.
So you film a walkthrough, shoot a Reel, post a few clips, run a listing ad, maybe boost it…

And it gets views. Engagement. Maybe even leads.

But here's the trap:

Your listing is the star.
Not you.

And once the home is sold, your visibility disappears with it.

You spent all that time marketing a property—but not your business.

Don't get me wrong: listings are useful.
But they should be used to draw attention to your system, not just the house.

You want people to think:

> *"If I ever list my place, I want this agent to do it."*
> *"This agent clearly has a process."*

That's the difference between marketing a property… and marketing *yourself*.

Myth #4: "I just need more exposure."

A lot of agents think if they could just get more visibility—more impressions, more clicks, more eyeballs—then the business would come.

But that's not how people make decisions.

Exposure without context is just noise.
Being seen doesn't mean being understood.
And being understood is what creates action.

You don't need more people looking at you.
You need the right people seeing the right message at the right time—when they're in a position to act.

Myth #5: "I have to be everywhere."

There's this pressure to show up on every platform: Instagram, TikTok, YouTube, LinkedIn, Facebook, Twitter, Threads...

But being "everywhere" quickly turns into being nowhere in particular.
You're stretched thin, your content is watered down, and your message is inconsistent.

Presence without purpose isn't visibility—it's busywork.

What actually moves the needle is being *strategic*—understanding where your ideal clients are, and showing up in ways that earn trust, not just attention.

Myth #6: "I need to prove I'm an expert."

Agents often lean on stats, market updates, and industry jargon to sound knowledgeable. It's well-intentioned—but it misses the mark.

People don't hire based on who sounds the smartest.
They hire based on who makes them feel understood and confident.

Being an expert matters—but it's how you communicate that expertise that counts.
Not through data dumps, but through stories, relevance, and emotional clarity.

Your value isn't just what you know.
It's how you make people feel about working with you.

Myth #7: "The more leads, the better."

Most agents chase volume. More clicks. More names in the CRM. More people at the open house.

But more leads is only a good thing if they're the right leads.

One serious, ready-to-act buyer is worth more than 50 cold ones who filled out a form and forgot about it.

What you need isn't more traffic—it's more traction.

A high-volume lead gen strategy without follow-up, filtering, or timing just creates noise.

Action-Based Branding focuses on quality—*because quality is what actually closes.*

Myth #8: "People will reach out when they're ready."

Maybe. But probably not to you.

Most people don't do "deep research" when they're ready to act—they go with who's already on their radar.

If you're not part of the conversation before they make a decision, you likely won't be part of it at all.

Being the first person they feel connected to—that's the goal.
And that's what Action-Based Branding does.

You're not just waiting for a lead to fall in your lap.
You're showing up early—building trust before the moment of decision arrives.

Myth #9: "If I care enough, they'll choose me."

Caring is the minimum. It's not a strategy.

It's true—your clients want someone who cares.
But if that care is invisible, it doesn't count.

You may want to help people—but your marketing has to show them that you can.
Not through self-promotion, but through relevance and value.

Marketing isn't about pretending to care.
It's about letting people feel that you do—before they ever meet you.

Myth #10: "Marketing means selling myself."

No—it means helping people solve problems.

Many agents feel uncomfortable with marketing because they think it means "talking about yourself." So they avoid it. Or they water it down with generic content.

But good marketing isn't about you—it's about them.

It's not "Look at me."
It's "Here's how I help people like you."

Action-Based Branding flips the spotlight:

It moves you from self-promotion to strategic service.

That's how you become the obvious choice—without being pushy.

The Shift That Changes Everything

Every myth in this chapter leads to the same solution:

You don't need more tactics.

➜ You need a system.

➜ A system that generates leads and builds trust.

That's what Action-Based Branding is.

It's a framework that:

- Attracts the right people
- Builds the bond before they're even ready
- Nurtures trust over time
- And converts when the moment is right

Once it's set up, you don't have to reinvent the wheel every day.
It runs. It builds momentum. And most importantly—it brings people *to you.*

You stop reacting… and start attracting.

Let the others burn out doing it the old way.

You're going to do it smarter.

CHAPTER 3: THE BOND

Why they choose you—and why they don't.

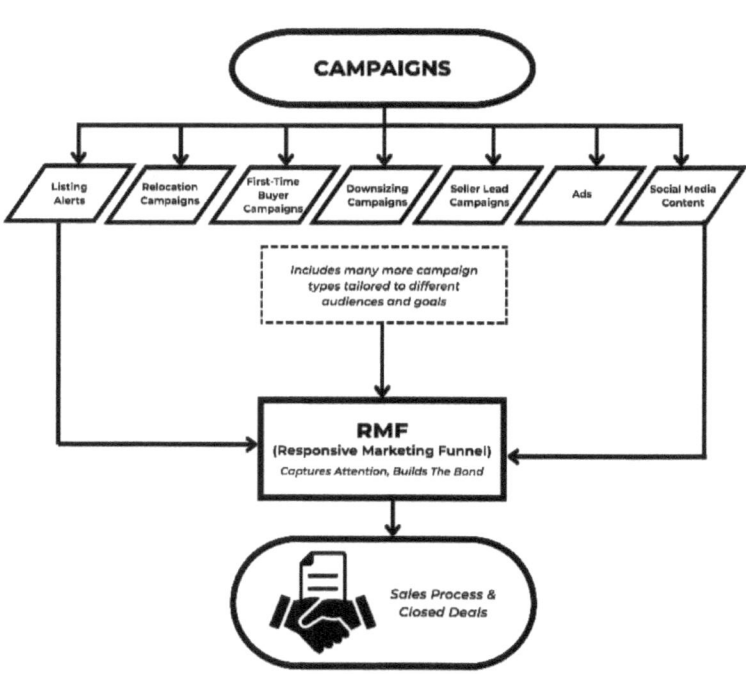

Let's talk about what actually closes deals.

It's not your listing presentation.

It's not your Instagram feed.

It's not your CRM.

It's the bond.

The bond is the emotional connection that makes someone choose *you*—before they've even met you.

It's what makes them feel like *you're the one* who gets it. The one they trust. The one they're willing to follow through a high-stakes decision.

And if your marketing isn't creating that bond?
Then all your effort is just noise.

In this chapter, we're going to break down how the bond works, how it fits into the larger sales process, and how Action-Based Branding systematizes it—so you can close more deals without chasing anyone.

1. Why the Bond Is Everything

People think clients choose based on logic—price, experience, reviews.

But they don't.

They choose based on *trust*.

And trust is emotional.

> They need to feel like you understand them.
>
> They need to feel like you've done this before.

They need to feel safe.

That feeling is the *bond*.

And in today's world, that bond is often built *before* the first conversation.

Through your marketing. Your messaging. Your presence online. Your follow-up. Your tone.

That's why the bond is everything.

Because the person they trust first is usually the one they'll hire.

2. Marketing Is a Two-Step Process—But It's Not the Sales Process

Let's separate the noise from the nuance.

When we say "marketing," most agents think we're talking about lead generation. Ads, social media, postcards—anything that gets your name out there.

But good marketing is more than just getting seen.

It's a two-step process:

> ***Step 1: Get Noticed***
>
> This is visibility. It's how people find out you exist.

You can get attention with ads, videos, content, open houses—whatever puts you on their radar.

Step 2: Get Chosen

This is positioning. It's why someone picks you over everyone else.

It's built through familiarity, consistency, relevance, and trust.

Most agents stop at Step 1.

They run an ad or boost a post, get a few clicks, and then wonder why no one calls back.

But Step 2 is *where the money is*.

Because when someone chooses you before the conversation starts—when they already feel like they know what to expect—you've already won half the battle.

And here's the proof:

According to the National Association of Realtors, 72% of buyers and sellers work with the first agent they talk to.

Not the best one.

Not the most experienced.

The first one who felt right.

That's why this second step—being the one they choose—is everything.

And here's the key part:

Marketing is what gets you in the room. Sales is what happens once you're there.

But once you're in the room?

You've already done more than half the work.

The hard part—getting someone to trust you enough to take that first step—is done.

They've seen you. They've heard your message. They chose to reach out.

Now?

All you have to do is help them—by actually helping them.

    Ask good questions.

    Listen more than you talk.

    Guide them to what they already want.

If you setup Action Based Branding correctly, you won't need to convince or push.

You just need to show up as the professional they already believe you are.

Because the bond is already there.

You're not chasing the deal.

You're simply closing the loop.

3. The Escape to Arrival Framework

Nobody moves just because they feel like it.
Even when it looks like a simple upgrade on the surface, there's always something deeper driving the decision.

Real estate is never just physical.
It's emotional. It's mental. Sometimes even spiritual.

A client might be chasing peace, freedom, security, identity, or status.
They're leaving something behind—and trying to arrive at something better.

That's the foundation of the *Escape to Arrival Framework*.

This framework helps us understand people in motion—people who are making real, emotional decisions—and translate that insight into marketing that resonates, attracts, and builds trust.

It's not just a mindset—it's a messaging tool.

How to Use the Framework in Your Marketing

The core idea is simple:

Every message you put out should speak to one of two things:

1. What your ideal client wants to escape

2. Where they're trying to arrive

When you get clarity on those two points, you unlock messaging pillars that feel personal, powerful, and persuasive.

You're no longer just advertising features.
You're speaking to feelings.

These pillars become the foundation for your:

- Ads

- Emails

- Landing pages

- Open house scripts

- Social content

- Brand voice

Examples:

If you're a Beverly Hills agent, your prospective clients may have just achieved financial success—but want their lifestyle to reflect it.

Your message could sound like:

- *"You've built success. Now it's time to live like it. "*
- *"Escape the noise. Arrive at the lifestyle. Here's how."*
- *"You've earned the view. Here's how to get it."*

If you're targeting first-time buyers, the focus is often financial freedom and self-respect:

- *"Tired of paying your landlord's mortgage?"*
- *"From renter to owner—what no one tells you."*
- *"Escape the lease. Arrive at ownership."*

If you're working with downsizers, it's often about peace, simplicity, and freedom:

- *"Escape the upkeep. Arrive at ease."*
- *"You don't need a bigger house. You need more life."*

These are just a few quick examples—we'll dive deeper into campaign-specific messaging later in the book.

The goal here is to illustrate the point:

You build the bond by showing that you understand where someone is—and where they want to be.

You're not selling them a house.
You're showing them that you *see* them—and that you've helped people like them get to the other side.

When your messaging aligns with their emotional journey, you earn trust *before* the first conversation.

And that trust—that *bond*—is the difference between a cold lead... and a warm conversation that turns into a client.

Why This Framework Works

People don't buy based on square footage.
They buy based on how they believe life will feel after the move.

The Escape to Arrival Framework gives you a structure to speak directly to that belief—without sounding like every other agent.

It shifts your messaging away from specs and stats...
and toward identity, desire, clarity, and momentum.

And when you do that right?
You're not just promoting a property.
You're narrating someone's next chapter.

That's how you attract people who are already in motion.

That's how you make your brand resonate.

That's how you build a bond before you even meet.

CHAPTER 4: THE ACTION-BASED BRANDING SYSTEM OVERVIEW

Everything we've talked about—The Bond, the two-step marketing process, and the Escape to Arrival journey—comes together here.

This isn't just a philosophy.
It's a system.
One you can set up, repeat, and scale.

We call it the **Action-Based Branding System**—a framework built specifically for real estate agents who want consistent, qualified leads without chasing cold traffic every day.

Here's what it looks like:

1. Campaigns: Like a Politician, Not a Content Calendar

Let's clear something up:
Campaigns aren't new.

You've probably run some version of one before—whether it was a new listing post, an open house, or a seasonal newsletter.

But what we're doing here is changing how you think about campaigns (and giving it steroids).

Most agents treat marketing like a content calendar or to-do list:

> "Post a reel today."
> "Send an email blast."
> "Upload a market stat slide."

It's reactive. Random. And exhausting.

But if you think of it like a political campaign, everything clicks into place.

A politician doesn't post randomly.
They campaign when it matters most—during election season—and they show up strategically and repeatedly, with targeted messaging for specific groups of voters.

Your real estate campaigns work the same way.

You're not marketing for attention.
You're campaigning for trust.

The more you campaign, the more people you "touch."
You're increasing your name recognition. Your visibility. Your perceived authority.

And just like with elections—you don't need everyone to vote for you.

You just need the right people to feel like you're their obvious choice when the time comes.

Examples of Campaigns You Can Run

Campaigns aren't limited to just ads or posts.

They can take many forms depending on your market and audience:

- An open house that's part of a larger awareness push
- A Facebook ad campaign designed to generate buyer leads
- A TikTok series answering common homebuying questions
- A LinkedIn content series aimed at professionals relocating for work

Each one serves a purpose. Each one builds your brand in a different way.

And here's the truth:

The more campaigns you can run, the better.

We'll go into even more examples later in the book.

But for now, just remember this:

Stop thinking like a content creator.
Start thinking like a candidate.

The campaign is your moment to show up, speak directly to what matters, and earn trust before you're even asked for help.

But here's where most agents fall short:

They launch a campaign... and then let it die.
No follow-up. No system. No momentum.

The problem isn't the campaign—it's the lack of a process that catches and converts the interest it generates.

Running campaigns without a system is like collecting votes and never counting them.

All that effort, wasted.

So how do you make sure your campaigns actually lead to deals?

You connect them to something bigger.

You integrate every campaign into a single, powerful engine that turns curiosity into conversations, and conversations into contracts.

In the next section, I'll show you how to do exactly that—
with the one tool that brings all of your campaigns together:

The Responsive Marketing Funnel.

2. **The Responsive Marketing Funnel (RMF): Your Digital Foundation**

If your campaigns are the speeches, rallies, and big promises… then the Responsive Marketing Funnel (RMF) is your field game—sometimes called the "ground game" in politics.

Now, I'm not a political strategist.
But from what I understand, the ground game is where elections are won.

It's the part that happens *after* the rally.

Follow-ups. Data tracking. Personal touches.

It's what happens after the attention is captured.
Not just getting people hyped—but getting them to show up and take action.

Your RMF works the same way—just fully digital and completely automated.

Here's the idea:

Most agents run a campaign… and then hope.

> Hope the lead remembers.
> Hope they follow up.
> Hope something sticks.

The RMF doesn't rely on hope.

It's a system designed to respond to what your lead is actually doing—and then gently guide them to the next step.

If someone browses listings in a specific neighborhood?
They get more homes in that area.

If they watch your video about downsizing?
They get a follow-up email with your "Empty Nester's Guide."

If they click a seller ad but don't convert?
They get retargeted across the web with a free home value offer.

Everything is intentional.
Everything is tailored.
And the best part? It all runs quietly in the background.

What the RMF Actually Does

The Responsive Marketing Funnel isn't complicated.
It's just a smarter way to stay in the conversation without chasing people down.

Here's what it does:

- It shows people what they're already looking for.
- It follows up automatically when someone shows interest.
- It reminds them you're here when they're ready.

- It guides them to take the next step naturally.

No pressure.

No spamming.

Just being helpful—and present—at the right moment.

You don't need to be a tech genius to implement this. I will show you how in Chapter 6.

The Responsive Marketing Funnel speaks directly to the people who are ready—and keeps the conversation going when they're not.

This is how your campaigns become compounding assets—not just one-off promotions.

The RMF ensures you're not just generating attention.
You're capturing it. Nurturing it. Converting it.

And because it's the central hub of your entire marketing system, we've dedicated a full chapter to breaking it down in detail later in this book.

Once it's running, your funnel becomes a digital version of you— *always present, always consistent, always building trust.*

3. The Sales Process: Turning Trust into Closings

If your campaigns are the rally, and your RMF is the ground game…
then the sales process? That's Election Day.

It's the moment of decision.

But if you've implemented Action-Based Branding the right way, this moment isn't stressful—it's natural.

You're not "selling" anymore.
You're confirming what the client already believes:

> *"This is the person I want to work with."*

That's the power of showing up before they're ready to act—with relevant campaigns, a responsive follow-up system, and messaging that builds trust.

By the time they meet you in person or hop on a call, there's no cold start.
No trying to prove your value.
No awkward small talk.
Just a sense of familiarity—and forward momentum.

Chapter Recap: Trust Wins Deals

Everything you've just read leads to one core idea:

Trust is what closes deals—and your marketing should be building that trust before you ever meet the client.

When you get this right:

- Your campaigns generate attention from the right people
- Your system follows up automatically
- Your meetings feel like a continuation, not a cold start

This is what Action-Based Branding is designed to do:

> Build the bond.
> Earn the vote.
> And make the sales process feel effortless.

In the next chapters, we'll take you deeper into the heart of this system.

You've already seen how the RMF connects with Campaigns and your Sale Process.

Now, let's break it down piece by piece—so you can build one that works while you sleep.

CHAPTER 5: THE BOND AND THE SALES PROCESS

Why trust wins deals—and why your job gets easier with the right system.

You Already Know What to Do From Here

This is where your strengths take over.

This is your zone.

You know the contracts.
You know your market.
You know how to guide people through the biggest transaction of their life.

All the technical parts—the disclosures, timelines, negotiations—that's where your expertise shines.

Action-Based Branding isn't about replacing that.
It's about *getting more people to go through your sales process.*

It's about getting more qualified, motivated people to your version of Election Day—and making sure they already feel like you're the obvious choice.

When that's in place, your job becomes less about convincing… and more about helping people take the final step they already want to take.

That's not cold outreach.
That's **confident alignment.**

No Script Can Save You Without the Bond

You can have the best listing presentation.
The most polished pitch.
The cleverest closing lines.

But if there's no bond?

You're selling uphill—and you'll probably lose.

The bond is the real differentiator.
It's the emotional groundwork that no script can replace.

The Big Shift: From Chasing to Responding

If you implement Action-Based Branding correctly, everything changes:

Instead of chasing lukewarm leads or trying to "convince" strangers...

You'll simply respond to people who have already raised their hand.

You'll be walking into sales conversations where:

- They already want your help.
- They already see you as the obvious choice.

It stops feeling like selling.
It starts feeling like **helping**.

Why the Bond Makes Decisions Easier

When the bond is strong:

- Clients feel less anxiety.
- They make faster decisions.
- They shop around less.
- They trust your advice more easily.

It doesn't matter how good your scripts are.
Without the bond, you're starting uphill.

With the bond, you're guiding someone who already sees you as the clear path forward.

Sales Resistance Drops When the Bond Is Already Built

Most sales resistance comes from uncertainty:

- "Can I trust this person?"
- "Will they pressure me?"
- "Do they get what I need?"

Action-Based Branding answers all of that **before the first handshake**.

Your content, your follow-up, your messaging—they've all been working together behind the scenes to build the bond.

By the time the meeting happens, your job is simple:

- Listen.
- Advise.
- Guide.

That's it.

You're not convincing.

You're aligning.

Once You Nail the Sales Process... It's Just a Math Game

Here's the best part:

Once you have your Sales Process dialed in, all you need to do is **flood your RMF with more people**.

More qualified leads

→ More people bonding with you automatically

→ More ready-to-act clients at your door.

Sales becomes predictable.

Growth becomes mechanical—not emotional.

The Machine That Powers It All

The Sales Process is critical.

It's the bread and butter of your business.

It's where your skills—advising, negotiating, closing—truly shine.

But here's the truth:

You can't win if you don't get enough people into the process.

The real game is **getting more qualified people to the starting line**.

And you can't build those relationships manually, one by one. You need a system that does it at scale—consistently, predictably, automatically.

That's what the **Responsive Marketing Funnel (RMF)** is built for.

In the next chapter, we'll break down how the RMF captures attention, builds trust automatically, and fills your calendar—without you chasing every lead manually.

Let's dive in.

CHAPTER 6: THE RESPONSIVE MARKETING FUNNEL (RMF)

Your Own Zillow

We're in a new era of real estate.

Buyers and sellers no longer wait to talk to an agent before taking action.
They start online.
They self-educate.
They browse listings at midnight and request info before ever talking to a human.

If your brand doesn't show up—and follow up—at the exact right moment, you're out of the conversation before it even begins.

That's why you need a *Responsive Marketing Funnel*.

The RMF isn't just a tool. It's your infrastructure.
It's what ensures you don't lose leads between "interest" and "action."
It's what builds trust while you're doing something else.
And in today's market, it's not optional—it's survival.

What This Chapter Covers

In this chapter, we'll break down the RMF from the ground up:

- What the RMF actually is (and why most agents don't really have one)
- Why relying on social media or a basic website is no longer enough
- The 3 essential parts of every effective RMF
- The psychology behind lead nurturing—and how to use it to your advantage
- How to build a funnel that's personalized, automated, and scalable
- Real-world examples of what this looks like in action

By the end of this chapter, you won't just understand what an RMF is—

You'll understand why it's the backbone of every modern real estate business that's winning right now.

This is how you scale trust.
This is how you multiply your time.
This is how you stop chasing and start attracting—at scale.

1. Why You Need a Responsive Marketing Funnel (RMF)

And why most agents don't even realize they're losing deals until it's too late.

Let's follow Linda.

Linda lives in the suburbs. She's thinking about moving closer to the city for work. Nothing urgent—just a feeling.

It's 9:47 PM on a Tuesday.
She's sitting on her couch with a glass of wine, and she picks up her phone.

She searches:

> *"2 bedroom condos near downtown Vancouver"*

The first result?
Zillow.

She clicks. She scrolls.
She taps through a few listings.
One catches her eye. She clicks again. Then she hits a wall:

> *"Enter your info to get more details."*

She hesitates—but she's curious.
So she enters her name and email.

Zillow now has Linda.

And what happens next?

Zillow sells that lead to the highest-bidding Realtor.
Someone who didn't build the bond, didn't nurture the lead, didn't earn the trust.
Just paid to be in the right place at the right time.

Meanwhile, *you*—a Realtor in Linda's market—were never in the conversation.

You lost the lead before you even knew she existed.

This Is Why You Need an RMF

The RMF is what puts *you* in that moment.

It's what gives Linda a better experience—on *your* platform, not Zillow's.

When she searches, she should find your site.
When she clicks, she should see your listings.
When she wants more info, it should be *you* following up.
Not a stranger she didn't choose.

This isn't just about lead capture.
This is about taking back control—from platforms that profit off your listings and relationships.

What the RMF Actually Is

The RMF isn't complicated.

It's not about fancy tech.

The RMF is your personal Zillow, built to serve you—not sell your leads to someone else.

It's a system that:

- Shows people the listings and information they're already searching for
- Follows up naturally based on their behavior
- Builds trust automatically—without you chasing them down
- Guides them toward working with you when they're ready

No cold calls.

No awkward "just checking in" emails.

No hoping they remember you.

You stay present, helpful, and top of mind—without feeling pushy or desperate.

Just like Zillow captures millions of buyers without picking up the phone...

Your RMF captures the right people—and brings them into *your* world.

Zillow Is Proof This Works

Zillow made over $2.2 billion last year by giving people what they want:

Listings.

They didn't close any deals.
They didn't show any homes.
They didn't negotiate one contract.

They just built a funnel that turned clicks into commissions—by selling leads to agents like you.

So if every client starts by looking at listings…
Why wouldn't you give them what they want—directly from *you*?

Zillow *Is* an RMF—Now You Need Your Own

That's what Zillow really is:
A massive, nationwide Responsive Marketing Funnel.

It captures attention, nurtures leads, and sells those leads to agents who didn't do any of the work.

So the question isn't *if* an RMF works.
The question is: Do you want to keep paying for someone else's RMF… *or build your own?*

But How Can I Compete with a Multibillion-Dollar Company?

Good question. And here's the honest answer:

- The bad news: Zillow is ahead of us.
- The good news: Zillow can't be you.

They're a platform. *You're a person.*
They're national. *You're local.*
They're generic. *You're specific.*

You can build an RMF that speaks directly to your market—your neighborhoods, your buyers, your sellers, your story.

Zillow can't do that. They have to be everything to everyone.
You only need to be the right person for the right leads in your zip code.

And here's the kicker:

Zillow already did the hard part.
They proved this works. They trained consumers.
Now all you have to do… is show up as the better option.

The RMF Is How You Compete

This is how you take your power back.

The RMF helps you:

- Get found earlier in the decision process
- Build trust through behavior-based follow-up
- Stay top-of-mind without chasing
- Capture more opportunities—*before* they hit Zillow

In the digital age, attention is easy.
Relevance is everything.

And the Responsive Marketing Funnel is how you become the relevant choice—before the client ever picks up the phone.

2. The Entry Point: Where the Journey Begins

Every Responsive Marketing Funnel starts with a single moment:

> A person raises their hand.

That "hand raise" can look like:

- Clicking a Facebook ad
- Watching a full TikTok video
- Signing up for a buyer's guide

- Browsing listings on your website
- RSVPing to an open house

The entry point is where attention turns into opportunity.

But not every entry point is equal.
What matters is **how aligned it is with intent**.

If someone clicks a listing ad and views three homes in a certain area, they're showing more buying signals than someone who just liked a generic "new listing" post on Instagram.

That's why your funnel doesn't start with "getting famous."
It starts with **capturing signals** from people who are actually in motion.

And your RMF's job is to meet them where they are—and guide them the rest of the way.

The Real Secret: People Want to See Listings

Let's stop pretending.

Clients don't care how many homes you sold last year.
They don't care how long you've been in the business.
They don't even care about your credentials—*at first*.

They just want to look at listings.

That's where the relationship starts.

And if they can't browse listings easily on your platform,
if they hit a wall, or feel like they're being pitched too early—
they'll leave and go back to Zillow.

That's why your RMF starts with **giving people what they actually want.**

Once you have their attention—**then you can build the bond.**
Then you can show your value.
Then you can earn their trust.

But if you lead with your stats or awards…
you're answering questions they're not asking yet.

3. The Follow-Up: What Happens Next Is Everything

Here's where most agents drop the ball.

They get a lead and don't follow up.
Or worse—they follow up with a canned "Are you ready to buy/sell?" message that pushes people away.

But the RMF is different.

It's not about pressure—it's about presence.

The RMF delivers the next message based on what the person just did.
That's why it feels natural. Personal. Relevant.

If someone checks out a downsizing video, the next step might be a checklist:
"5 Signs It's Time to Right-Size Your Life."

If someone clicks a relocation guide, you don't pitch them—you send:
"Here's What to Know Before You Move to Vancouver."

It's soft. Helpful. Trust-building.

And it all happens automatically.

This is the *responsive* part of the funnel.
It responds—not just sends.

That's the difference between follow-up and **follow-through**.

4. When It All Works

When your RMF is built properly, here's what happens:

A buyer in your market clicks on your content.
They land on your RMF and finds listings that matches what they're looking for.
They browse, click, engage.

You follow up—based on what they actually care about.

They feel understood.

They feel seen.

They reach out.

And here's the kicker:

You never had to chase them.

You were already there.

And once that system is in place, it runs like a machine.

You don't need to be a tech wizard.
You just need to know your market—and show up in the right way.

5. Why the RMF Changes the Game

You can't scale hustle.
You can scale a funnel.

The RMF is how you move from **hustling for leads** to **receiving qualified conversations**.

It doesn't just save time.
It builds a pipeline that gets stronger every week.

It frees you up to focus on the part you're best at—advising, negotiating, closing—while the front end of your business runs in the background.

If you want a business that works when you don't, this is it.

It's not optional anymore.

It's the foundation and the future of real estate marketing.

And now that you understand it…

Let's talk about how to get more qualified leads into your RMF.

CHAPTER 7: CAMPAIGNS AND ENTRY POINTS

How to flood your RMF with opportunities.

Campaigns Are Your Invitations

Most agents treat marketing like a chore.

"Post something."
"Send a postcard."
"Boost an Instagram reel."

It feels random. Exhausting. Unrewarding.

But campaigns change everything.

A campaign isn't just a post.
It's an intentional **invitation**—designed to make the right person raise their hand.

Campaigns are how you create *movement* in your business.
They're how you get people out of browsing mode and into decision mode.

And the more invitations you send?

The more hands you catch going up.

Entry Points = Doors Into Your System

Every campaign you run creates an **entry point** into your world.

- A Facebook ad offering early access to new listings?
  Entry point.

- A QR code at your open house that offers a free relocation guide?
  Entry point.

- A TikTok video breaking down the hidden costs of renting vs buying?
  Entry point.

Each entry point feeds your **Responsive Marketing Funnel**.
Each one gives your system someone new to nurture, educate, and guide.

No entry points, no leads.
More entry points, more opportunities.

It really is that simple.

Why You Need Many Campaigns (Not Just One)

Most agents run one campaign at a time—and wonder why leads trickle in.

They post one open house.
They boost one video.
They hope it works.

But here's the truth:

You don't need one viral campaign.
You need multiple steady campaigns.

Not every campaign will explode.
But when you have multiple campaigns quietly running in the background, feeding your funnel?

You build *predictability*.
You build *momentum*.
You build a business that doesn't collapse when one thing underperforms.

Examples of Campaigns That Work

Here's where it gets fun.

You're not limited to "just listed" posts or boring newsletters. You can (and should) run campaigns like:

- **Listing Alerts**:
  "See homes before they hit Zillow—Get VIP access."

- **Relocation Campaigns**:
  "Moving to Beverly Hills? Download the Ultimate Relocation Kit."

- **First-Time Buyer Campaigns**:
  "Everything You Wish You Knew Before Buying Your First Home."

- **Downsizing Campaigns**:
  "5 Signs It's Time to Right-Size Your Life."

- **Seller Lead Campaigns**:
  "Find Out What Your Home Could Sell for in Today's Market."

- **Open House Funnels**:
  QR code + signup form → instant follow-up

Each one creates a **specific door**.

Each one talks to a **specific moment** in the buyer or seller journey.

Each one brings people into your RMF ready to be nurtured.

The Real Secret to Every Campaign

There are literally millions of ways to campaign.

You could run:

- First-time buyer ads
- Luxury open house tours
- Relocation checklists
- TikTok explainer videos
- Instagram story polls
- Facebook carousel ads
- YouTube neighborhood guides
- Open Houses
- Just meeting new friends at a social event
- Talking to your cousin who lives in another neighbourhood

We could sit here and list campaign ideas all day long.

But the truth is:

It's not about what type of campaign you run.
It's about where every campaign leads.

Whatever campaign you choose to run, the goal is the same:

Always send people back to your Responsive Marketing Funnel (RMF).

Every ad, every video, every email, every conversation— should make it easy for someone to find your listings, your brand, and your follow-up system.

Even at the end of your emails, you should always include a link to your RMF.

At the end of an open house, if someone asks:

> *"Are there other similar homes in the area?"*

You don't need to fumble for an answer.

You can simply say:

> *"Absolutely. If you'd like, I can send you a private list later today— or you can visit my site now and see all the latest listings in real time."*

And guess what?

Those listing links better come **from your RMF**.

Because every time you send people back into your funnel, you're building momentum.
You're building familiarity.
You're building trust.

You're not just answering questions—you're **strategically guiding them deeper into your world**.

That's how you stop chasing leads—and start controlling the conversation.

The 72% Advantage

Why does this matter so much?

Because according to the National Association of Realtors:

72% of buyers and sellers hire the first agent they meet.

Not the flashiest agent.
Not the cheapest agent.
The first one they feel comfortable with.

Every campaign you run…
Every entry point you build…

Is another chance to be the first agent someone meets.

And when you're first, you're often the last.

The Hidden Secret Behind Winning Campaigns

Let's be honest.

The real secret to getting leads isn't your branding, your years of experience, or how many homes you've sold.

It's listings.

That's what people care about first.
That's what they search for late at night.
That's what triggers curiosity and action.

Not your awards.
Not your market reports.
Listings.

And successful agents know this.

They don't try to sell themselves first.
They give people what they already want: ***access to homes (digitally first).***

Give the People What They Want

So instead of shouting "Top Producer!" or "20 Years of Experience!"...

Give the people what they want.

Show them homes.

Show them what's possible.

Make it easy to browse, dream, imagine.

Because when they're finally ready to make a move?

The only Realtor they'll think of is the one who's been helping them from the very beginning—you.

How Zillow and Top Agents Dominate the Internet

You know who else figured this out?

Zillow.

And the top agents who quietly dominate online.

The real magic happens through **Google**.

When someone starts dreaming about moving, what's the first thing they do?

They Google it.

"Homes for sale in Beverly Hills."
"Best neighborhoods in Vancouver."
"How much house can I afford?"

Remember Linda from our earlier chapters?

The first thing she did was open Google and search for "Beverly Hills real estate."

And who showed up first?
Zillow.

If you had a Responsive Marketing Funnel connected to Google—whether through paid ads or smart SEO—you could have been the first agent Linda interacted with.

You could have captured her attention before Zillow ever got a chance.

The One Campaign You Can't Ignore

You don't have to run 20 campaigns to win.

But if you're serious about competing in today's market?

You must show up on Google.

Whether through paid search ads, smart content, or organic strategies—
Google is where the majority of buyer and seller journeys begin.

If you don't exist there?

You're invisible when it matters most.

If you're only going to focus on one channel first, *make it Google.*

Own the search.

Own the mindshare.

Own the relationship.

Because when someone searches, you want your brand—not Zillow's—to be the first thing they see.

Campaigns Are a Compounding Asset

The real power of campaigns isn't what happens today.

It's what happens 3 months, 6 months, 12 months from now.

Because when you keep creating entry points:

- Your database grows.
- Your audience warms up.
- Your brand becomes the familiar, trusted option.

Campaigns don't just create leads.

They create **momentum.**

And momentum is what separates agents who hustle endlessly from agents who *scale effortlessly*.

Open More Doors—and Keep Them Open

At this point, your system is almost fully built.

You have:

- A clear Sales Process.
- A bond-building strategy.
- A Responsive Marketing Funnel ready to nurture.
- Campaigns and Entry Points feeding your funnel.

Now your job is simple:

Keep opening doors—and make sure people keep seeing them.

Because here's the truth:

Most people won't act the first time they see your campaign.
Not because they're not interested—
but because life gets busy, timing isn't perfect, or they need a little more warming up.

And that's where **Retargeting** comes in.

In the next chapter, you'll learn how to stay in front of your audience—without spamming, begging, or feeling desperate.

We'll show you how to gently guide people back into your world—until they're ready to take action.

Because marketing isn't just about opening doors.

It's about keeping doors open long enough for the right people to walk through.

Let's dive into Retargeting.

CHAPTER 8: RETARGETING – HOW TO STAY TOP OF MIND WITHOUT BEING ANNOYING

Stay visible. Stay relevant. Stay trusted.

Why Retargeting Matters

Most people don't take action the first time they see you.

Not because they're not interested.
Not because you did something wrong.
Simply because *that's how real people behave*.

They get distracted.
They need time to think.
They need more exposure before they feel ready.

Studies show it often takes **7+ touches** before someone is comfortable enough to take action.

That's what Retargeting is about:

Staying gently present while your future clients warm up.

What Retargeting Really Is

Retargeting isn't stalking.

It's not blasting people with ads until they're annoyed.

It's not chasing.

Retargeting is simply reminding people you exist—at the right moments.

When done right, Retargeting feels like:

- A friendly reminder
- A familiar face in their feed
- A reassuring nudge when the timing is finally right

How Retargeting Fits Into Your System

Every Entry Point you create…

Every campaign you run…

Every click or visit you get…

Should trigger a retargeting journey.

Because if someone showed enough curiosity to click once?

They're 10X more likely to convert later—**if you stay present.**

The Responsive Marketing Funnel (RMF) is built to handle this.

Retargeting simply ensures you're using your RMF to its full potential.

Simple Retargeting Examples

You don't need complicated tech to start.

Here are easy ways to retarget:

- Facebook Retargeting Ads (to people who visited your website)
- Google Display Retargeting (showing ads to past visitors)
- Email Drip Campaigns (to people who downloaded your guide)
- Text Message Follow-Ups (to Open House leads)
- YouTube Video Retargeting (to people who watched part of your tour videos)

Each touchpoint is a soft reminder:

"Hey, I'm still here when you're ready."

The Key: Stay Helpful, Not Pushy

Good Retargeting always feels helpful.

Bad Retargeting feels spammy.

Here's the simple rule:

☑ Focus on adding value (sending more listings, helpful tips, local market updates)

☑ Avoid pushing them before they're ready (no "Are you buying yet??" messages)

If you do it right, you're not pestering.
You're patiently staying in the background—until they step forward again.

Retargeting Turns "No" Into "Not Yet"

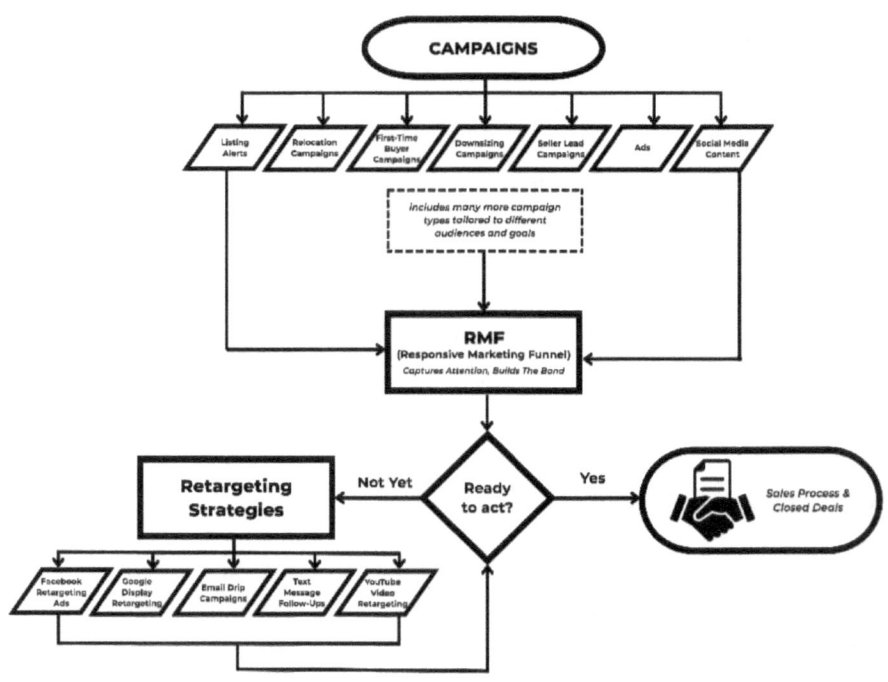

Every click that didn't turn into a lead?

It's not a no.

It's a *not yet.*

Retargeting is how you turn "not yet" into "let's go."

You don't lose leads—you simply give them time to come back when they're ready.

CHAPTER 9: CONCLUSION AND FINAL WRAP-UP

Building a business that brings clients to you.

Where You Started vs Where You Are Now

When you started this book, you were probably doing what most agents are taught to do:

- Post more.
- Chase attention.
- Stay "top of mind."
- Hope something sticks.

You were working hard—no doubt.
But chances are, you were working too much for too little.

Now, you know the truth:

You don't need more attention. You need more action.

You don't need to chase leads.

You need a system that **attracts and nurtures them**—until they choose you naturally.

What You Now Have

You now have a complete system:

- **A Sales Process** that's natural and trust-based—not pushy.

- **The Bond** built before the first meeting—even before the first call.

- **The Responsive Marketing Funnel (RMF)** to nurture leads automatically, while you focus on real conversations.

- **Campaigns and Entry Points** to constantly invite new people into your world.

- **Retargeting** to keep you visible and trusted without being annoying.

You don't have to wonder what to do anymore.

You have a machine.

Now all you have to do is **turn it on**.

What to Focus On First

You don't need to build the perfect system overnight.

Start simple:

- One Campaign.
- One Entry Point.
- One RMF connected to it.

Get one door working.
Then build another.

Action-Based Branding isn't about perfection.

It's about momentum.

Small wins compound.
One lead becomes three.
Three leads become six.
Six leads become a waiting list.

Just start.
And keep building.

The Real Secret to Winning

The agents who win aren't louder.

They're smarter.

They understand:

- People want listings, not lectures.
- People want trust, not pitches.
- People want guidance, not pressure.

Marketing becomes easy when you stop chasing and start serving.

Be visible.

Be valuable.

Be available when they're ready.

And you won't have to compete—you'll already be chosen.

Final Encouragement

You're not just learning how to market better.

You're building a business that:

- Attracts the right people.
- Builds trust automatically.

- Closes more deals with less stress.

- Grows without burning you out.

You already know how to help people move.

Now you have a system that moves people toward you.

This is the future of real estate marketing.
And you're ready for it.

Let's build it.

---

www.ingramcontent.com/pod-product-compliance
Lightning Source LLC
Chambersburg PA
CBHW030445220526
45464CB00006B/2421